Turtle in July

by **Marilyn Singer**

illustrated by **Jerry Pinkney**

Macmillan Publishing Company   New York

Collier Macmillan Publishers   London

Macmillan Publishing Company
866 Third Avenue, New York, NY 10022
Collier Macmillan Canada, Inc.
Printed and bound in Hong Kong
First American Edition

10   9   8   7   6   5   4   3

The text of this book is set in 13 point Meridien.
The illustrations are rendered in pen and pencil with watercolor on paper.

Library of Congress Cataloging-in-Publication Data
Singer, Marilyn.
Turtle in July.
Summary: An illustrated collection about the
activities of particular animals in each month of the year.
1. Animals—Juvenile poetry. 2. Months—Juvenile
poetry. 3. Children's poetry, American. [1. Animals—
Poetry. 2. Months—Poetry. 3. Seasons—Poetry.
4. American poetry] I. Pinkney, Jerry, ill. II. Title.
PS3569.I546T87   1989   811'.54   89-2745
ISBN 0-02-782881-6

Title calligraphy by Leah Palmer Preiss

BULLHEAD IN WINTER

 in winter
I sleep
  belly down in the shallows
below me
  mud
above me
  ice
next to me
 on either side
  bullheads asleep
  belly down in the shallows
below them
  mud
above them
  ice
next to them
 on either side
  bullheads asleep
  belly down in the shallows

January Deer

I am a January deer,
so swift and light
the hard-packed snow does not even
   crunch
beneath my hooves.
While others around me
sleep in silent caves,
   I run
through the white world
   with wide-open eyes.

Barn Owl

February night
    (sweep)
Thick clouds
No moon
    (search sweep)
Soft snow
No ice
    (hush sweep)
Patience
Silence
Wait for the
    (sweep)
    squeak
Now swoop
    snatch
    crack
A hard time for owls
But harder still for mice

Deer Mouse

get   get get get   get
  get
    out of the nest
  get
    into the cold
get   get get get
  get
    food
    lots of food
  get
    seeds
    berries
    nuts
    bugs
    bark
get enough to last
get enough to store
get more
get   get get get   get
  get going
    move
      hustle
don't rustle
don't squeak
    beware
    danger in the air
get busy
get done
get   get get get
  get out of here
    run

BULLHEAD IN SPRING

in spring
I spawn
    belly down in the shallows
where no trout
    no whitefish
    no salmon
    can go
I lay
    one two three four
       thousand eggs
my mate and I watch them hatch
             hatch
    in the warming mud
little black bullheads
    swimming free
      to new mud
        new shallows

March Bear

Who I?
  Where I?
When I now?
  No matter
Need water
Few berries
Fresh ants
  Not so hungry
Or am I?
Don't think so
  Not yet
And anyway it's too early for honey
Funny
That odor
  This river
That hollow
  This den
I know them
  Well, sort of
I've been here
  But when?
  No matter
New morning
Remember it then

april is a dog's dream

april is a dog's dream
the soft grass is growing
the sweet breeze is blowing
the air all full of singing feels just right
so no excuses now
we're going to the park
to chase and charge and chew
and I will make you see
what spring is all about

Myrtle Warblers

Me me me
I am
me me me
See the yellow yellow yellow
   on my wing-ing-ings
Me me me
I am
me me me
I'm the fellow fellow fellow
   here who sing-ing-ings

May May May
It is
May May May
Come and pair up pair up pair up
   you and me me me
May May May
It is
May May May
Meet me there up there up there up
   in that tree tree tree

Hi hi hi
I say
hi hi hi
I think your voice your voice your voice
   is the best best best
Hi hi hi
I say
hi hi hi
You are my choice my choice my choice
   Come, let's nest nest nest

BULLHEAD IN SUMMER

in summer
I eat
   belly down in the mud
 moving slow and easy
I find
   worms
 and water beetles
   pondweed
 and snails
   dragonflies
   alderflies
   crayfish
 and side swimmers
over my head
 a turtle passes by
I don't bother him
he doesn't bother me
 good summer neighbors

Cow

I approve of June
Fresh food to chew
  and chew
  and chew
Lots of room to move around
  or lie down
Not too hot
Not too cold
Not too wet
Not too dry
A good roof of sky over me and my calf
Who's now halfway up
  on new legs
He'll want a meal real soon
Yes, I approve of June

Turtle in July

Heavy
Heavy hot
Heavy hot hangs
Thick sticky
Icky
But I lie
Nose high
Cool pool
No fool
A turtle in July

Dragonfly

Look
   skim
      there
         snap
            eat
Repeat
Look
   skim
      there
         snap
            eat
Repeat
Look
   skim
      there
         snap
         hey
It got away
Look
   skim
      there
         snap
         oh
Where'd that one go?
August slow?
For a dragonfly
         no
Look
   skim
      there
         snap
            eat
Repeat

BULLHEAD IN AUTUMN

   in autumn
I settle
     belly down in the shallows
above me
    leaves
      red and yellow
   spinning slowly
     in the wind and water
on the shore
    a lone fisher
      casts a line
  begging me to bite
don't waste your time, fisher
  it's autumn
    and in autumn
I settle
    belly down in the shallows

Timber Rattlesnake

Summer it still is
   Yes
September stones
Warm bones
Warm blood
Strike I still can
    Yes
Snare and swallow the harvesting mouse
                 the shuffling rat
But slant they do the sun's rays
Shorter grow the days
   Yes
Soon September stones
Chill bones
Chill blood
Stiff shall I grow
And so below I'll slide
Beneath stones
Beneath soil
Coil I still can
    Yes
Sleep safe
Sleep sound
Snake underground

Canada Goose

Did I tell you?
I should tell you
Going home
We're going home
Are you coming?
Yes, you're coming
Going home
We're going home
How the sun will warm each feather
How the wind will make us fly
Follow me—I'll be your leader
As we flap across the sky
Are you ready?
I am ready
Going home
We're going home
Is it time now?
It is time now
October's happened
And we're going home

Beavers in November

This stick   here
That stick   there
   Mud, more mud, add mud, good mud
That stick   here
This stick   there
   Mud, more mud, add mud, good mud
      You pat
      I gnaw
      I pile
      You store
This stick   here
That stick   there
   Mud, more mud, add mud, good mud
      You guard
      I pack
      I dig
      You stack
That stick   here
This stick   there
   Mud, more mud, add mud, good mud
      I trim
      You mold
      To keep
      Out cold
This stick   here
That stick   there
   Mud, more mud, add mud, good mud

Cat

I prefer
warm fur,
a perfect fire
to lie beside,
a cozy lap
where I can nap,
an empty chair
when she's not there.
I want heat
  on my feet
   on my nose
   on my hide.
No cat I remember
dislikes December
  inside.

FOLGER McKINSEY ELEMENTARY SCHOOL